simpleSolutions

Storage Space

simpleSolutions

Storage Space

COLEEN CAHILL

Foreword by Timothy Drew
Managing Editor, *Home Magazine*

FRIEDMAN/FAIRFAX

A FRIEDMAN/FAIRFAX BOOK
© 2002 by Michael Friedman Publishing Group, Inc.

Please visit our website: www.metrobooks.com

Library of Congress Cataloging-in-Publication Data

Cahill, Coleen.
    Storage space / Coleen Cahill.
        p. cm. – (SimpleSolutions)
    Includes bibliographical references and index.
    ISBN 1-58663-307-4 (alk. paper)
        1. Storage in the home. 2. Built-in furniture. I. Title. II. Series.

    TX301 .C23 2002
    648'.8—dc21

                                                    2001058580

Editor: Rosy Ngo
Art Director: Jeff Batzli
Designer: Orit Mardkha-Tenzer
Photography Editor: Lori Epstein
Production Manager: Richela Fabian-Morgan

Color separations by Fine Arts Repro House Co., Ltd.
Printed in China by C & C Offset Printing Co., Ltd

10 9 8 7 6 5 4 3 2 1

Distributed by Sterling Publishing Company, Inc.
387 Park Avenue South
New York, NY 10016
Distributed in Canada by Sterling Publishing
Canadian Manda Group
One Atlantic Avenue, Suite 105
Toronto, Ontario, Canada M6K 3E7
Distributed in Australia by
Capricorn Link (Australia) Pty, Ltd.
P.O. Box 704, Windsor, NSW 2756 Australia

Acknowledgments

Thank you to Tim Drew from *Home Magazine* for contributing the foreword, and to Lori Epstein and Rosy Ngo from Friedman/Fairfax.

Contents

FOREWORD   6

INTRODUCTION   8

CHAPTER ONE: Living and Working Spaces

Media Storage   10

Shelf Space   20

Decorative Displays   26

Home Offices   32

Clean and Organized   42

CHAPTER TWO: Kitchens

Cabinets Galore   50

Cooking Conveniences   58

Surprise Storage   66

Creative Food Storage   72

Out in the Open   76

Auxiliary Areas   80

CHAPTER THREE: Bedrooms and Baths

Containing Clutter   84

Space-Saving Ideas   88

Clothes, Shoes, and More   98

Just for Kids   104

Within Reach   110

Shared Spaces   116

Freestanding Flexibility   120

GARAGE, ATTIC, AND BASEMENT TIPS   124

RESOURCES   125

INDEX   128

Foreword

Have you ever wondered whether in ancient Rome, Julius and Julia Q. Publicum sometimes came home from a shopping trip to the Forum and complained that they didn't have enough space to hang up his new Calvinus Kleinus toga or to stow those oh-so-stylish Gucchicum sandals she'd found on sale? Or, when Sir Francis Drake finally returned to London after his adventures on the high seas, did he discover that his home office just couldn't accommodate all of his maps, charts, and navigational instruments, much less all those lovely souvenirs and mementos that travelers seem to accumulate? Oddly, history books totally overlook the crucial evolution of walk-in closets, bookshelves, linen closets, pantries, kitchen cabinets, bathroom vanities, and the like.

On the other hand, there is no doubt that people now just have a lot more stuff—clothes for any and all occasions and seasons, sports and hobby equipment, electronic entertainment and business paraphernalia, small appliances, and, of course, an ever-expanding array of grooming products and sundries, to cite just a few examples.

These days, we don't have to be spendthrift instant-gratification-seeking shopaholics to conclude that if we don't get organized soon, we'll become overwhelmed and doomed to be eternally trying to find something. Have you ever experienced the frustration of rooting through clutter, trying to find those suddenly needed financial statements or the coriander you remember buying last week for that new recipe? Or worse, we completely forget that we even have specific things, never mind where they might be (think of the great sweater your sister gave you for your birthday the year before last).

Knowing that you are on the brink of chaos is great motivation for getting a grip on what you own. And, believe it or not, there are really only two main rules for taking control. The first rule is to be honest with yourself and decide what goes and what stays. (Are two espresso machines really necessary? Is even one needed if it's never been used?) Donating extra goods to charity is both liberating and gratifying. The more you pare down, the sooner you'll see a faint glimmer at the end of the tunnel.

Don't start feeling too smug, however; after you've edited your belongings down, you'll need to call up all of your perseverance and sense of purpose, plus a healthy dollop of creativity. Deceptively simple-sounding, the second dictum is "a place for everything and everything in its place." Now that you've culled through overstuffed closets, cabinets, and drawers, it's time to really think about what should go where and what kind of new storage equipment or furniture you may need. You'll want to consider convenience and accessibility. This can be a staggering quest, but fortunately simpleSolutions: *Storage Space* offers you a complete outline of how to resolve all those storage problems you thought were hopeless. With so many inspired ideas and plenty of photos to show you how it's done, your home will have a place for everything with everything in its place.

Timothy Drew
Managing Editor, *Home Magazine*

Introduction

It's impossible to go through life without accumulating a few belongings along the way. That's part of the fun! Coming across the perfect souvenir to bring home from a faraway land or spotting an antique plate that's been missing from your collection can deliver a powerful sense of joy. When we bring objects—whether new or old—into our homes, they become part of our lives. They tell stories about the places we've visited and the experiences we've shared. Though invaluable, our prized possessions are only a small fragment of the objects that compete for space in our homes. Everyday items like food, clothes, and books are more plentiful, and are an integral part of our lives.

No matter how big your home is, there never seems to be enough room for everything you own. Large homes may appear to have a natural advantage when it comes to storage, but the amount of space devoted to storage isn't the most critical issue. It's more important to make sure that you have the kind of storage that suits your home and family.

Lifestyle and the size of your family will influence your storage needs. When thinking about storage solutions, consider the activities and hobbies of the entire family. Children can be counted on to accumulate all sorts of stuff as they pass through phases from toddlerhood to adolescence—even little babies require sizable equipment like strollers and swings. On a smaller scale, books can take over a room as quickly as bulky athletic gear. You can't predict the passing fancy of each family member, but try to anticipate the types of materials that will need to be stored before mapping out storage plans for your home.

Personal preference is another important consideration when planning storage. Are you a minimalist who appreciates a clean, spare room? Or, do you like to display your collections? Your approach to storage will be influenced by the type of environment you feel most comfortable in, and by the design of your home. For example, an older home may have smaller closets than a newly constructed home, but high ceilings and spacious bedrooms present other storage opportunities that can make up the difference.

If you're planning to build a new home, make storage an important part of your plans right from the start. Do you have the space for walk-in closets in the master bedroom? Do you need a mudroom? Ask yourself what you'll store in the mudroom—coats, shoes, school backpacks, or sporting equipment. Consider a built-in entertainment center to organize electronics, or incorporate a separate home office into your plans.

Whether your home is new or old, storage should be tackled one room at a time. Nearly every room needs some type of storage, but there are a few hot spots.

The kitchen is one of the most important rooms in the home and a true storage center. When planning kitchen storage, think about the types of foods that need to be stored and the way you like to cook. Do you use lots of fresh ingredients? Do you have a large array of spices, oils, or vinegars? Are you a serious cook with a large collection of pots and pans that need to be within easy reach? Food preparation and storage may still be a kitchen's primary purpose, but today these rooms often do double duty as family rooms, offices, or homework centers. So think about what activities take place in your kitchen and how they will affect the storage you need.

The bathroom is another critical space for potential storage. Bathrooms have gotten larger in the last few decades, but storage areas within them have not necessarily followed suit. Think about who will be using the space—a couple, guests, or kids. The layout and amenities may be different for each group, and storage requirements will vary, too. Adequate space for towels and toiletries is the foundation of bathroom storage, but a host of other items—from hair dryers to cleaning supplies—can add to the clutter. Safety and accessibility are two other concerns that should be given priority when planning and organizing bathroom storage.

One of the main culprits of bedroom mess is our own clothing. Culling your wardrobe is one of the best ways to get a handle on bedroom organization, where a well-equipped closet is the key to a tidy room. Closets are the main storage area in the bedroom, and—depending on the type of clothes and accessories you have—can be outfitted with a combination of drawers, shelves, hanging poles, racks, and more. Many of today's bedrooms also feature a desk area or a place to relax with a good book. So, some of the storage challenges we face in other areas of the home apply to the bedroom, too.

Throughout the rest of the home, some of the most common sources of clutter are books, magazines, CDs, and DVDs. A combination of open and closed storage will allow you to display some things out in the open, while hiding more unsightly items behind closed doors. In living areas, storage can be an integral part of the design of the room, even becoming a decorative focal point. Solutions that are both functional and stylish are the best way to go.

A good way to ensure that storage solutions are tailored to your home and family is to take stock of everything you have—from baby clothes you're saving to dust-covered golf clubs in the garage. One of the most critical steps in storage planning doesn't involve storage at all. At least twice a year, get rid of the possessions you no longer want—give them away to a charity or have a yard sale. It will make you feel better and will make organizing your home much easier.

Once you're left with what you need to store, it's helpful to place items into categories and decide how frequently they are used. Then it's time to take a look at your home. Evaluate each room, including the attic, garage, and transitional areas such as hallways and under the stairs. Decide what storage features can be utilized as is and which spaces might require reorganization or additional pieces to increase storage capacity. If you need to increase the overall storage in your home, consider a combination of built-in solutions and freestanding pieces that provide flexibility.

simpleSolutions: *Storage Space* is the ideal companion as you begin to think about storage in your home. It contains specific solutions for different rooms and is filled with ideas that can help you uncover the hidden storage that already exists in your home. The most important step in creating an organized, clutter-free home is getting started. Good luck!

Coleen Cahill

Media Storage

Today's homes are equipped with more electronics than ever before, from large screen TVs to multi-disk CD players. Whether your family relaxes in an informal living room, family room, or den, there is an array of storage units that can house complete **home entertainment** systems, including smaller items—videotapes, DVDs, and CDs—that frequently turn into clutter. Custom or modular wall systems are popular, but a compact media cabinet will also do the trick.

At the center of a handsome wall unit, a cabinet holds a large TV, while shelves inset above contain the VCR and videotapes. Cabinets like these should have an open back or holes cut into the back panel to provide ventilation for the TV. Closed storage below conceals more equipment and electronic games, and can be easily accessed by children. ➲

Whether you want to listen to music, watch a movie, or curl up with a good book, this stylish storage unit accommodates a variety of media. A small desk provides a convenient place to work, while shallow glass shelves display delicate objects above. Glass doors on either side of both the stereo section and the TV section can slide out and close, screening off the equipment when not in use. ◑

A pullout, swivel shelf allows the TV to be viewed from anywhere in the room.

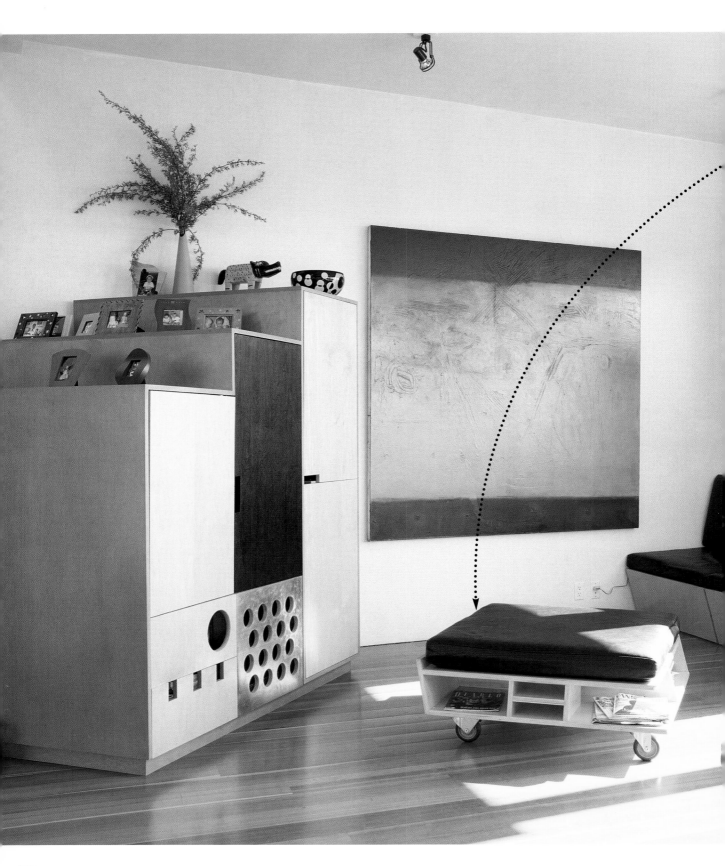

A contemporary ottoman doubles as a coffee table and storage for magazines.

A freestanding entertainment center is the focal point of this room. Placed on an angle, it's easily viewed from either banquette. The multilevel top surfaces serve as a display area for family photos. ☯

Doors slide in and out of the way to reveal a large TV and stereo components. Note the cut-out panels in the lower cabinetry, which holds additional speaker components. ☯

Making the most of otherwise wasted space, a window seat offers a cozy spot to relax plus convenient storage below. Cabinets open to reveal pullout shelves and a collection of CDs that can be viewed at a glance. ☊

Built-in speakers ensure superior sound while blending in with the shelving.

A sleek high-end screen commands a central position amid built-in shelving that creates a beautiful display. The simple, spare design of the shelving focuses attention on the featured entertainment, while additional equipment is concealed behind smooth cabinet doors. ➲

F orm and function marry, yielding a voluptuous design that features an undulating wall with an integrated fireplace and media storage. The TV is set into a niche at the top, while shelves below house the VCR and books. The stylish storage continues around the corner, where oversized books are stowed in a shielded cubby. ◖

P roving that storage can make a subtle design statement, these wall-mounted units are integrated into the architecture of the room. The industrial-inspired shelving pairs wood with brushed steel to create unobtrusive storage for smaller items like CDs. ◑

A floor-to-ceiling closet reveals an abundance of storage. Open shelves house the TV and other electronics, while drawers allow efficient storage for loose items. Placing boxes and baskets on the shelves is a good way to increase organization and maximize the storage possibilities for letters and photographs. ⊃

Closet doors close for a neat, finished, and uncluttered look. ⌒

Shelf Space

helves come in all different shapes and sizes, and are one of the most **versatile** storage options available. Built-in shelves can transform a living room into a library, and turn a tight corner into a clever storage space. Freestanding shelving units offer even greater **flexibility**—look for modular units with adjustable shelves, or expand your storage options by adding boxes, baskets, and bins. Remember that shelves designed for books and other heavy objects will need to be **sturdy.**

bright ideas

- Paint shelves a bright hue for a splash of color
- Recess shelves into the wall when space is an issue
- Consider opaque glass doors to obscure cabinet contents without closing in the space

Bins at the unit's base add a bit of enclosed storage.

Bookshelves are at their best when they are thoroughly integrated into the design of the room. Here, built-in blond wood shelves extend from the floor to the ceiling, creating an attractive backdrop for the contemporary furnishings. Books are interspersed with objets d'art, offering an open and visually appealing display. Another built-in touch is a library ladder that rolls along the length of the room, allowing for safe access to books on the upper shelves. ➲

A gold mine of storage is found in the space beneath these stairs. Instead of conventional hardware, two holes allow each cabinet to be pulled out and its contents revealed. ➤

Inside each cabinet, a separate set of shelves holds everything from linens to sporting equipment. Placing items that are used frequently—especially by children—within easy reach makes sense when there is storage at several different heights. ➤

Spiral stairs leading up to a study and an adjacent wall are turned into an ad hoc library with floor-to-ceiling shelves filled with books. Peruse titles on the climb up and relax at the top with your selection. ∩

keep in mind

☐ Consider the maximum height and reach for shelves and storage units:

Maximum suggested
shelf height:
72" (184cm)

Maximum drawer height:
55" (140cm)

Maximum reach for women:
77" (196cm)

Maximum reach for men:
83" (211cm)

Nesting woven baskets add playful color to a dark bookc
and are the perfect home for loose items. ☊

Though we don't live in transitional spaces like stairways, we pass through them several times a day, making them a convenient place for storage. Here, otherwise unused space is transformed by built-in shelves that climb up with the steps. ➲

No space goes unused—shelving continues around to the top of the stairs.

A pair of bookshelves takes advantage of the space on either side of pocket doors. A clever system of doors allows a limited section of the books to be viewed at one time, since a single large door may have been unwieldy. ↻

Decorative Displays

Storage can also take on an **ornamental** function. Special decorative objects or collections can add a personal touch to a room, and should be showcased where they will be enjoyed. The objects themselves—their shape, color, or fragility—may influence how they are displayed, and the **style** of the room is another factor to consider. Whether you desire built-ins that lend a room a traditional air or a sleek, freestanding piece, there are plenty of **beautiful** ways to show off your prized possessions.

bright ideas

▶ Turn the space above windows and doorways into display areas

▶ Display plates and other collectibles on shallow, grid-like shelves

▶ Showcase special or one-of-a-kind objects in recessed niches

The fireplace is the focal point of this room, and the arched niche above it is fitted with shelves for display purposes. An array of ceramic collectibles stands out against the white shelves, while the decorative molding frames the niche and sets it apart from the surrounding wall. Molding is used throughout the room, and helps integrate the bookcases to the left of the fireplace into the room. ↻

This wet bar area and built-in shelf unit—stained a complementary warm, honey tone—becomes part of the room's comfortable architecture. A gentle arch defines the bar area, while two architectural columns anchor the space. Open shelving is perfect for the collection of American pottery displayed throughout the room. Stemware is on view (and within easy reach) behind glass cabinets. ↻

Smaller pieces in the pottery collection are displayed on the shelf above the window.

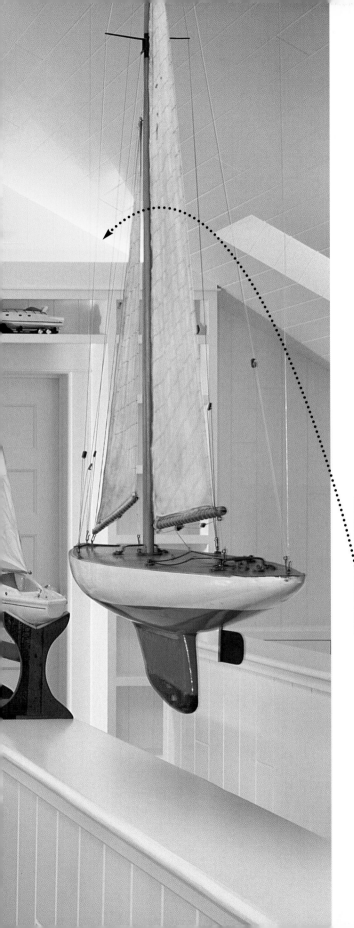

An extensive collection of model boats resides in custom-designed "berths" that turn a hallway into a gallery. Tailoring shelves and cubbyholes to their contents creates a more integrated display. Here, larger boats are showcased along the bottom in bigger cubbyholes, while smaller models are displayed at the top. Oversized vessels that defy such confinement are placed atop the shelving, and are instead framed by the peaked ceiling. ☾

Spotlights bring the decorative display to life.

The traditional bookcase gives up its straight lines for the sake of panache. A curvaceous version offers contemporary display for artwork, cut flowers, potted plants, vases, and books. This wavy unit also serves as a stylish yet purposeful room divider. ☊

Now you see it, now you don't. Bleached maple doors that slide back and forth to reveal—or hide—your treasures are especially appealing features of this attractive cabinet. When you don't want to overshadow the existing decor, a partially open-shelved unit that lets the wall's stormy hue show through is ideal. ➲

Home Offices

Turn an extra room or a small alcove into a **workspace** by converting it into a home office. A desk and comfortable chair are the only necessities, but drawers, cabinets, and shelves will all come in handy when it's time to get down to work. Careful planning is the key to creating a fully **functional** home office. Even if you don't work from home, a well-organized place to pay bills or catch up on correspondence is a great use of extra space.

bright ideas

▶ Tack up notes and reminders on corkboard (cover it with fabric for added charm)

▶ Outfit drawers with rods for hanging files

▶ Install locks on drawers that hold important documents

A small leaf pulls out, creating a convenient spot to rest a book for easy perusal.

Plenty of built-in storage enhances an organized and tidy workspace. Located directly behind the desk, a grid of open storage is both attractive and functional. Reference books are within easy reach, while an adjacent built-in unit features additional open storage with drawers below for files and supplies. ➲

Drawers deep enough for hanging files are a must in a serious office area.

Making the most of a corner space, built-in desk furniture forms an extremely efficient work area. The granite countertop provides a smooth work surface, while overhead cabinets and drawers below hold files and office supplies. The corner was designed specifically for the computer and offers plenty of legroom. ☊

Situate your home office in a location where you'll enjoy working. This windowed alcove provides a view of the greenery outside, which means that overhead cabinets must be limited to the adjacent wall. However, the expansive L-shaped counter offers plenty of work surface and creates room for closed storage below. ○

This compact workstation has everything you'll need to enhance your productivity. Increasing desktop storage, a four-drawer hutch designed specifically for desks with computers rests on the surface. A desk lamp makes use of the space atop the drawers, while the pullout tray houses the keyboard, mouse, and mouse pad to keep the desktop clear. ☾

Beware of harmful dust when placing your CPU near the floor—a clever little trolley gives the computer enough lift to keep it safe.

When space is limited, think about expanding vertically. A colorful, compact desk features a hutch rising from the desktop. Tall legs leave room for a computer monitor, while storage compartments above house books, accessories, and a few decorative items. ☊

Another vertical touch— wicker drawers keep paperwork and smaller items organized.

Vertical magazine files are a simple and inexpensive way to preserve magazines for future reference, and come in a variety of colors and patterns for a decorative touch.

Capacity and functionality of a simple bookcase is expanded with a colorful collection of storage devices. Blue in/out trays and a wicker basket atop the shelves organize current paperwork, while chartreuse drawers on the shelf below house office accessories. ◖

Depending on your line of work, a home office may have special storage features tailored to your particular needs. A short staircase that leads to an artist's studio offers the perfect place for flat files. Deeper drawers on the left and cabinets above provide room for paints, vessels, and other art supplies. ➲

Flat files are the perfect place for stowing neatly organized tubes of paint, special papers, and prints. ◖

Express your personal style in your home office. The simple lines of this desk are contrasted with curvaceous chairs and the cylindrical form of the desk lamp. An open storage unit along the wall has an architectural feel while drawing the eye upward to nesting boxes and the plant placed on top. The simplicity and uniformity of the items on the shelves add to the overall attractiveness of the room. ☊

A substantial desk and chair are the focal point of this home office. The light-filled room has the advantage of floor-to-ceiling closets along one wall, which comprise the bulk of the available storage. Inside, they have been fitted with built-in drawers and shelves, but when the doors are closed, the office is clutter free—except for an attractive display of books on the lower shelf. ↻

Clean and Organized

udrooms, entryways, and laundry areas are the unheralded heroes of the house. In these functional spaces, you can discard soiled garments, such as gardening gloves and shoes, and ensure that you will have something **clean** to wear. These spaces rely on **well-organized** and **accessible** storage to do their jobs. Plus, you need enough room to complete the task at hand, whether that's folding clothes or lacing up a pair of boots. Be **utilitarian** when it comes to storage!

bright ideas

▶ Consider heated floors for mudrooms (choose slip-resistant and waterproof surfaces)

▶ Mount wooden dowels at an angle for drying boots

▶ Install wire or screen shelves for drying mittens, hats, and scarves

Simple furnishings can turn an entryway into a functional space. A wall mirror has a display shelf with five hanging pegs for hats, light jackets, even flippers. The bench provides storage beneath the seat, as well as a spot to sit while getting ready to head outdoors. ➲

A small stool provides a convenient place to sit or place a tote bag.

In this mudroom, open storage offers each person his or her own "locker." Cubbies get footwear off the floor, pegs hold coats and hats, and shelves above stow beach towels or winter sweaters. Everything has its place yet remains on view and easily accessible— the key to an efficient mudroom. ☊

If your home lacks a distinct mudroom, a large entryway can take its place. This mountain retreat has been outfitted with an assortment of hooks and racks that keep outerwear within reach of the entire family. A trio of baskets that fits into a hand-painted wooden frame keeps hats and mittens in a convenient place next to the door. Coats are accessible on the rack above the antique bench, which is a must for any entryway that serves as a staging area for the outdoors. ⬙

A functional place to stow boots, clothing, and accessories is a necessity for a rural lifestyle. The flagstone floor is an ideal choice to resist dirt and water, while an antique bench comes in handy as a place to pull on boots. Horseshoe hooks are sturdy enough for heavy jackets and chaps, while beadboard cabinets with wrought-iron hardware provide ample closed storage. ↻

A clever use of extra space, this narrow niche provides the perfect place to hang freshly laundered shirts.

With a bit of planning, a sunny space performs several functions, serving as a laundry room, mudroom, and potting shed. Permanent storage was sacrificed for increased functionality, making space planning the main concern. A smooth counter atop the washer and dryer provides a place to fold clothes, while the surface along the wall is dedicated to plants. ⌒

Transitional space just outside the kitchen is turned into a utility area thanks to two closets—one containing an ironing board and the other a washer and dryer. This convenient workstation allows clothes to be pressed as soon as they come out of the dryer. Stacking the washer and dryer is a smart space-saving idea. ◑

This storage system is attractive and utilitarian at the same time. The shelves—ideal for freshly laundered towels, linens, and a supply of soaps—are right where they are needed, directly above the granite counter that tops the washer and dryer. ⊃

A small utility sink is useful for washing delicate garments or soaking stained clothing.

In addition to permanent storage, a garment rack comes in handy in the laundry room. This one has wheels and can be easily moved around the house. ☊

Kitchens
Cabinets Galore

Proper storage is a must in the kitchen, and cabinets are a mainstay—called upon to house food, appliances, dishes, and cookware. There are a host of cabinet styles, materials, and colors to **choose** from, which, along with the layout, will greatly impact your kitchen's design. Whether you're considering custom or stock cabinetry, it's important to have a specific plan for your kitchen. Start with the location of the fridge, the stove, and the sink (the work triangle), and then **organize** your kitchen cabinets around the triangle.

bright ideas

▶ Install accent lighting above cabinets

▶ Mix and match hardware for an eclectic look

▶ Add vertical dividers to cabinets to organize trays, cutting boards, and baking sheets

In this kitchen, a classic L-shaped layout includes a variety of cabinet shapes and sizes, creating versatile storage options. Drawers on both sides of the oven provide a convenient place for cooking utensils, while slender glass-fronted cabinets flank open shelves to create a hutch-like display for vases, cookbooks, and more. ⌒

Matching refrigerator and freezer facades to the cabinet fronts creates an uninterrupted look throughout the kitchen.

An island is a popular way to increase the work and storage areas in a kitchen. This spacious, modern kitchen accommodates a sizable island with two cooktops, and cabinets below. The added storage on both sides of the island keeps pots and pans near the cooking area. ⌒

Take advantage of high ceilings if your home has them. This kitchen makes maximum use of the vertical space with cabinets stacked on top of each other. Within easy reach, glass-paneled cabinets hold everyday dishware and glassware. Way up by the ceiling, closed cabinets stow items that are needed less frequently. A step stool is a must with cabinets like these. ♪

A short peninsula with an overhang allows for an extra base cabinet and increases counter space, while providing a place for informal meals.

Create a wish list for your kitchen before selecting cabinets. On this homeowner's list were several clever storage features: a tamboured appliance garage that conceals the toaster and other small appliances, and below-the-counter wicker baskets that store vegetables. Early planning ensured that the baskets were properly integrated into the cabinets, sliding in and out easily. ↻

Making the most of limited wall space, a cabinet constructed largely of glass hangs in front of the kitchen window. The trees outside can be glimpsed, and light still flows into the room, filtering through the contents of the cabinet. ☊

For the quickest access to cabinets and drawers, select hardware that can be easily grasped.

Without sacrificing one bit of function, these cabinets make a supremely stylish statement. Stepped base cabinets echo the curve of the countertop, while a combination of drawers and shelves flank the cooktop. ☊

Expand the work area and storage capacity of your kitchen with a center island. Topped with granite, this generously proportioned unit features a built-in wine rack on one end with display shelves on either side created by angling the two corners. Along with roomy base cabinets, these built-in features enhance the functionality of this very attractive island. ☝

Glass-fronted cabinets showcase an attractive collection of dishware and glassware, while base cabinets and drawers stow the more utilitarian items. A see-through refrigerator allows you to locate drinks before opening the fridge. With this much glass in the kitchen, it's important to keep cabinet interiors tidy! ☕

Opening on both sides, these suspended cabinets are perfectly situated to conveniently provide access to dishware from either the kitchen or the dining room. ⌒

Cooking Conveniences

While today's kitchens are multipurpose rooms, they are still primarily **work centers** for preparing meals. When it's time to cook, the last thing you want is to waste time searching for the right pan. Plan ahead so that cooking essentials are conveniently located. Keeping utensils and cookware organized goes a long way toward creating a **smooth-running** kitchen. Think about designing a food prep area that reflects the way your family prepares meals—depending on whether you have one cook or two cooks in your family.

bright ideas

- ▶ Install wall-mounted metal railings or wire grids to hang utensils

- ▶ Hang overhead racks for easy access to pots and pans

- ▶ Integrate pullout or lift-up shelves for small appliances

Outfitted in brushed stainless steel, this light-filled galley takes its cue from commercial kitchens. Counter space is limited, so a small prep cart (on wheels for easy maneuvering) is called into action as a work surface. The cart features a drawer for utensils, and open shelves beneath store bowls and serving trays. Additional open shelves are found below the cooktop, and closed storage below the sink stows bulkier items. ⟳

Note the translucent backsplash, which offers protection without obscuring the light.

The extensive collection of pots and pans hanging from hooks above the professional-style range suggests that cooking is a serious affair in this kitchen. Plenty of counter space is a must, especially if there's more than one cook. Here, a substantial island is drawn up to the cooking area when it's time to prepare meals. Casters allow the island to be moved around the kitchen as needed, while cabinets below the work surface provide generous storage for bowls and more cookware. ◖

A kitchen wall without mounted cabinets is turned into a cook's pantry. Dried foods, grains, and snacks are displayed in air-tight mason jars on two shallow shelves. Below the shelves is a slender railing from which cooking utensils are hung. The expansive length of counter provides plenty of room for a long run of base cabinets below. ☞

Although this large kitchen has an abundance of cabinets and counter space, it lacks a center island to create a more efficient work triangle. Instead, a table is wheeled out from beneath the counter when needed and used as a work surface or a staging area for meals. This is a flexible, space-saving solution that allows traffic to move freely throughout the kitchen. ↻

When not in use, the table can be conveniently stowed beneath the countertop, with stools tucked right underneath. Deep cabinets with shelves that slide out make dishes stored in the back of the cabinet just as accessible as items stored up front. ☞

When space is limited, a freestanding drop-leaf cart is an ideal solution. This one offers three easy-access storage baskets (that glide smoothly on wood runners) and a single storage drawer with a handle that's ideal for hanging dish towels. Two extension leaves open up for a generous work surface and drop down to occupy minimal space when not in use. ↻

Cooking—not to mention cleanup—is made easier by a compost drawer. This one slides out from the side of a work island and has a removable metal tray ideal for transporting the contents outdoors. ➲

keep in mind

☐ A prep island featuring different levels and materials offers greater functionality

☐ Counters of different heights are appropriate for different tasks:

for everyday food prep—36" (91cm)

for rolling out dough—30" (76cm)

for chopping and cutting—42" (107cm)

To keep knives where you need them and still minimize countertop clutter, consider a butcher-block countertop with a recessed knife slot. Knives slide in easily, and the surrounding butcher block serves as a convenient cutting board. Be sure that the knife blades are completely covered when in their slots, so there's no danger of getting cut. ➲

Surprise Storage

typical kitchen contains variations of base cabinets and wall cabinets, but there are a host of other storage devices and **space-savers** that will help you stow all the things that a well-equipped kitchen needs. The first step in evaluating your storage needs is to take an inventory of your kitchen—include everything from appliances to cookbooks—and decide which items need to be stored. Then look for creative solutions that maximize space and convenience—and perhaps offer a surprise!

This tamboured appliance garage opens to reveal a toaster and a coffee machine. It's a simple way to take advantage of the space between the countertop and the cabinets above. ◑

Careful planning allows several compact storage solutions to be revealed with minimal effort: recessed shelves pull out to disclose an extensive collection of cookbooks; a convenient chopping board is disguised as a drawer; and an end cabinet slides out for access to appliances. ◐

The space above cabinets is useful as a display area.

Sometimes the best storage solutions are behind closed doors. Here, swing-out shelving installed in the corner section of a lower cabinet provides additional space for cookware and small appliances. It's a simple way to maximize an awkward space. ℃

A foldout cabinet at counter height is faced with bookshelves. It's a good idea to store cookbooks at eye level so that titles can be easily read, but that's just half the story with this cabinet. ↻

Open sesame! The bookshelf folds out to reveal more storage behind. This is a space-saving idea worth remembering. ⌒

Dropping down from beneath the microwave is a compact kitchen "desk." With room for paper, pens, and other office essentials, the divided tray keeps items organized and simply lifts out of the way when not needed. ☰

A handy tilt-out tray is a smart way to store sponges and scouring pads. Located close to the sink, but out of sight, simple solutions like this one keep counter clutter to a minimum. ☰

Store serving trays and baking pans in hard-to-reach kitchen cabinets since you probably don't need to use them every day. This cabinet, situated above the microwave, is fitted with vertical dividers that keep trays tidy. An added benefit is that you can remove one item without disturbing the others. ➲

Dividers can be added to existing drawers or built into new cabinetry. A wooden knife block provides individual slots for each knife, which helps prevent accidental cuts and keeps blades sharp (knives that brush against each other will grow dull). ➲

Creative Food Storage

ood storage is one of the most important features of every kitchen. Think beyond the traditional **pantry** when planning the food storage areas in your kitchen. Some foods are better preserved or more easily accessed when stored in dedicated compartments. Get started by considering the ideal way to store the various types of food you consume, from pasta and canned goods to produce and perishables. **Preserving** food is paramount, while accessible solutions will ensure that you can put your hands on the right snack or ingredient when you need it.

bright ideas

▶ Build slanted, self-feeding shelves for cans

▶ Ensure lids on metal- or plastic-lined drawers are secure to protect against moisture and pests

▶ Expand storage space with a foldout pantry

Metal-lined drawers inside this cabinet were designed to store dry ingredients such as flour and sugar. Each of the five drawers pivots to provide access and has a removable lid— a must! ➲

Modern appliances can make a traditional statement, too. In this classic kitchen, refrigerated drawers provide clever storage for ice-cold beverages and perishable food items directly under the counter. Storing food in smaller compartments lets you locate what you need quickly. ➲

Pullout pantry units take advantage of hard-to-reach spaces and slide out for easy access. Available in various configurations, this tall, narrow cabinet pulls out to reveal shelves chock full of boxed and bottled goods. The shelves are made of coated wire, which is easy to clean. ☮

Note the single strip of wood that holds items in place.

For tea lovers, a freestanding unit is divided into cubbyholes, each with a small wicker basket for teabags. Each basket contains a different blend so that the sachets are easily removed when it's time for a cuppa. ☊

A traditional wall pantry is outfitted with pullout wire baskets that hold potatoes and vegetables, while canisters store dried foods on the open shelves above. Another simple way to expand the capacity of a pantry is to mount shelves on the inside of cabinet doors. The ones here are ideal for smaller items. ☮

Out in the Open

Take an open approach to storage. Some items in the kitchen are best stored out in the open for all to see. Dishware, glassware, and other everyday items are ideal candidates for open storage since easy access is an **added bonus**. A favorite collection can add a personal touch to a kitchen and even become a decorative focal point of the room. Think about taking a few of your favorites out from behind closed doors.

An eclectic collection of white dishware creates a busy, yet charming, display. Keep in mind that shelving should be fitted to its contents— not the other way around. Staggered shelving in the center section accommodates taller pieces and adds visual interest. ➲

Simple hooks are screwed into the shelf to hang teacups.

The goal for this kitchen is an uncluttered environment. Even with open shelving, the minimalist look is achieved with neat stacks of dishware. The cabinets below conceal pots, pans, appliances, and other less decorative items. Both the slender shelves and cabinets follow the gentle curve of the exterior wall. ➲

The design and materials featured in this diminutive kitchen make it feel airy despite its size. The ceiling skylight fills the room with natural light, while the blond wood used throughout gives the illusion of expanding the space. Open glass shelves—which seem to float above the work area—were installed instead of cabinets. The five-shelf unit serves as a delicate divider and display area for colorful glass pieces. ◗

Open shelving in a modern design effectively creates a division between the kitchen and the dining areas, while maintaining a sense of spaciousness. Sleek cabinets with sliding doors conceal clutter at counter level. ↻

Auxiliary Areas

If you have the space, consider creating an auxiliary area in your kitchen, or in an adjoining pantry, for staging meals, storing wine, or paying bills. The extra surface will come in handy, especially if you like to **entertain**. Adding base or wall-mounted cabinets creates a discrete storage area that can be used for fine china, crystal, or serving pieces. Call it the new **butler's pantry**—minus the butler!

Ideal for presenting coffee and dessert, this attractive staging area includes an auxiliary sink that comes in handy during prep and cleanup. Cabinets extended from the main work area of the kitchen provide extra closed storage, while open shelving serves as an attractive display area for a collection of pottery. ➲

Note the tile backsplash to protect the wall from water sprays.

Located away from the main activity, a cheerful corner packs a lot into a small space. A compact work area provides a convenient place to peruse cookbooks and features a built-in corkboard for notes and reminders. A series of cubby-drawers provides tidy storage for odds and ends, while the cabinets above hold stemware. The selection of glasses comes in handy when it's time to access the wine refrigerator below. ↻

The countertop is illuminated from above. Adequate lighting is essential for every work surface.

Wine storage and a second dishwasher are concealed behind an attractive cabinet with doors that slide in and out of the way. The glass-fronted wall cabinets are dedicated to barware, while the countertop offers a smooth, uninterrupted surface for preparing drinks. ☊

A decorative woodcarving is an elegant touch.

keep in mind

☐ If you entertain frequently, outfit a butler's pantry with a second dishwasher, sink, and refrigerator

☐ Dishware and accessories required for serving large parties need special storage—an upper cabinet or shelving in a closet keeps pieces out of the way but still accessible

The handsome combination of wood, granite, and stainless steel turns this updated butler's pantry into a stylish beverage station. Open shelves keep stemware and tumblers within reach, while cabinets provide discreet storage. Wine enthusiasts will appreciate the extra capacity offered by a pair of refrigerated wine storage units below. ↻

Bedrooms and Baths
Containing Clutter

The bedroom should be a restful and relaxing place where the worries of the day recede. The key to ensuring that the bedroom remains **inviting** is organization. Everything from magazines and books to electronic equipment can slowly take over the bedroom. A good place to attack bedroom clutter is around the bed itself—headboards, nightstands, and foot-of-the-bed solutions keep belongings close at hand, yet out of the way.

bright ideas

▶ Place magazine racks by the bedside

▶ Buy a nightstand that includes drawers

Display space in this bedroom is consolidated in an attractive shelving unit on wheels. Since wall space is limited, the unit floats in the middle of the room, which helps to define the sleeping area. A small nightstand next to the bed holds essentials like an alarm clock and books. ➲

A wall of cabinets is an effective partition in this spacious bedroom. Open shelving serves as a headboard and takes the place of nightstands, providing plenty of room to stow reading materials. At the foot of the bed, a two-story bookshelf offers even more accessible storage. ↻

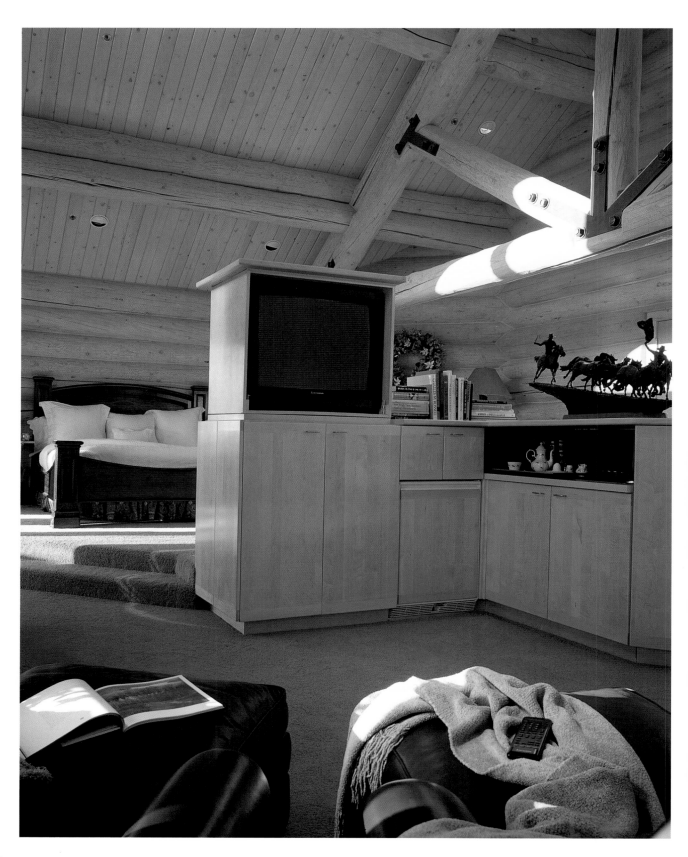

Having a television in the bedroom may not mean you want to see it all the time. This cabinet is full of surprises—when it's time watch a movie, the TV elevates from the cabinet below. When hidden away, there's no trace of it and the room is ready for restful activities like sleeping or reading. ☾

Offering a surface to place a reading lamp, a glass of water, and a current book, this handsome nightstand is more substantial than the usual bedside table. Deep drawers and a small cupboard provide space for nightclothes and other essentials. Expanses of wall between the shelving units and nightstand as well as open space at floor level furnish welcome visual breathing room. ☝

Space-Saving Ideas

he centerpiece of every bedroom, taking up the most space, is the bed itself. Built-in features—like a sleeping loft or Murphy bed—will **free up** floor space, but require up-front planning. Whether you have a guest bedroom that serves **double duty** as a den or a small master bedroom, there are plenty of space-saving solutions that combine sleep, storage, and more!

bright ideas

▶ Free up space with trundle beds

▶ Incorporate storage below benches and window seats

▶ Custom build drawers, shelves, and desks to fit into existing spaces

With the bed concealed in a built-in recess, this long, narrow guest room is ready for its day job. Cabinets above the bed store extra blankets and pillows, while those adjacent store guests' clothes and shoes. Oversized cubbyholes in the same blond wood as the bed and cabinets offer even more storage and complete the clean, organized look. ❍

With the bed lowered, the room turns into a comfortable sleeping alcove—
counter springs at the head of the bed allow for easy lifting and lowering. 🎧

keep in mind

☐ Check local codes before building a sleeping loft, which must be secure and sturdy

☐ The recommended minimum headroom above a loft bed is 4'6" (137cm), and 6'6" (198cm) for standing room below

It's hard to believe a mattress is concealed behind this bench, so complete is the transformation. Now the room is ready for music practice or other after-school activities. ◑

A ledge at the foot of the bed offers a place to sit while putting on shoes, or better yet, a spot to rest a breakfast tray.

This slim but useful bed folds into a bench during the day—an ideal solution for a guest room that has more than one role to play. Daybeds are another good choice for rooms that need to combine seating and sleeping into one piece of furniture. ◑

When space is limited, make the most of every square inch. Drawers integrated into the bed frame—a design traditionally known as a captain's bed—are a practical place to store clothes or bed linens. This modern equivalent to the seafaring storage unit is just as effective at freeing up space in closets and drawers. ○

A ceiling light and a pair of wall sconces illuminate the room and sleeping area. A small, circular window lets in a bit of fresh air and natural light.

This Arts and Crafts–inspired bedroom makes the most of a small space. A sleeping loft with built-in storage below creates extra floor space and eliminates the need for dressers. On one side, drawers are topped by a cabinet, while on the other side the space was left open for display purposes. ❍

High ceilings in this room allow for a built-in loft with copious storage. Access to the pair of twin beds above is via a sturdy ladder—a must with sleeping lofts. On either side of the ladder, large cabinet doors conceal shelves that hold clothes, toys, and more. ➲

A window seat offers a spot to sit plus additional drawers for storing extra pillows and linens in this charming guest bedroom. Deep closets flanking the window seat create the sidewalls for a cozy feel. ➲

One piece of furniture defines an entire sleeping area. This platform/ storage unit accommodates a double mattress and contains significant storage potential. Opening toward the bed, cabinets store clothing, while shelves mounted to the ceiling house books. The floor unit also acts as a room divider, separating the sleeping area from the living space. ☞

This all-in-one solution packs a lot of storage into one piece with drawers below the sleeping platform, too. Note the substantial drawer pulls for easy access. ☝

Proving that storage can be stylish, a sleigh bed is outfitted with a single drawer that pulls out from the foot of the bed. An ideal place to stow extra linens and throws, the slim drawer keeps contents neat and organized. ⬆

What appears to be a wall of floor-to-ceiling cabinets is not. A Murphy bed is hiding behind the large doors on the left, while on the right a small leaf lowers to create a tidy workstation. ➲

Clothes, Shoes, and More!

he most important storage area in the bedroom is the closet. Keeping your closet organized is the key to **maximizing** storage space. Walk-in closets offer the most significant space, and can be fitted with a combination of shelves, drawers, hanging poles, and racks. With a little planning, smaller closets can be filled with features that rival a walk-in. Decide which type of closet organization works best in your bedroom, then think about the categories of clothes and accessories that you need to store, and how much room to allow for each article. Don't forget about storage for seasonal clothing!

bright ideas

▶ Install tie or shoe racks on backs of doors

▶ Combine full-length and half-height rails in closets

▶ Use hooks and pegs for light-weight items

A wall closet is transformed into an old-fashioned wardrobe thanks to pullout drawers for smaller items like socks, and shelves above for folded shirts. A mirror has been hung on the inside of the door for one final check—a simple solution worth remembering. ➲

A slender dresser provides additional drawer space convenient to the closet.

Sometimes two closets are better than one. This pair is customized with built-ins to suit his and her particular needs. Her closet includes plenty of cubbies for shoes and open shelves for folded clothes, while his features drawers and a double row of hanging poles for jackets. Custom solutions can be designed to suit the specific needs of everyone from kids to parents. ☊

No detail has been overlooked—even bottles of cologne have a home.

An attic space has been converted into a Douglas fir-lined dressing room. With enough space for his-and-her areas, identical dressers have been built into the wall beneath the sloping eaves. In between, a double dresser provides even more drawer space and a surface for accessories and a small lamp. With this many drawers, seasonal clothes can be stored in the same location all year. ☊

A stool comes in handy to reach upper shelves and as a place to sit while putting on shoes.

Custom-built cabinetry transforms this otherwise shallow closet, making the most of an awkward corner space. A narrow cupboard has been designed with open shelves for sweaters and drawers below in varying depths. This frees up the shelf above the clothes rack for extra blankets. ☊

This is the kind of closet that could turn anyone into a clotheshorse! Large enough to function as a dressing room, this space is also filled with special features. Thin shelves store folded shirts fresh from the cleaners, while elongated pegs are draped with trousers. ☊

Bamboo blinds diffuse the natural light to prevent clothes from fading.

Combining style with outstanding function, this closet is meticulously organized. It succeeds in showcasing an entire wardrobe at a glance, which streamlines the morning rush. Three tiers of pegs for trousers and a double row of hanging poles comprise the main section of the closet. A series of small cabinets line the room, while a collection of hats is stowed in open shelves above the full-length clothes rack. ☉

keep in mind

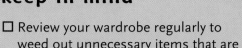

☐ Review your wardrobe regularly to weed out unnecessary items that are taking up valuable space

☐ Plan to rotate your wardrobe seasonally, stashing off-season clothing in an out-of-the-way place

In older homes, closets are often limited or missing altogether, and freestanding pieces have to pick up the slack. Here, a handsome wardrobe provides abundant storage behind closed doors, while an antique trunk at the foot of the bed stores blankets, sweaters, and other bulky items. ☉

Just for Kids

Storage is essential in a child's bedroom that also serves as a playroom and homework center. Finding the room to store clothes, books, and toys requires planning, organization, and a little **creativity**. Think about creating zones within the room for studying, playing, and clothes storage. Then focus on the type of storage that will help organize each area to ensure an **efficient** use of space. Good storage will help kids enjoy their rooms fully—and help keep the space clean and tidy, too!

bright ideas

▶ Color-code crates and bins for hobby supplies and toy storage

▶ Double hang rods to maximize closet space; place in-season clothes on the bottom within reach of children

Storage around the bed is a good way to contain clutter. Here, a headboard with built-in shelves keeps books organized and within easy reach for bedtime stories. A matching desk provides a dedicated workspace for crafts or homework. It can also fit a computer in the future—look ahead when planning children's storage. ⌒

Adjustable shelves are fitted with cleverly-designed bookends.

Effective storage doesn't have to break your budget. An affordable study area features an array of useful components starting with a sturdy desktop with pullout keyboard tray. Coated wire drawers keep notebooks and supplies handy, while wall-mounted shelves hold books and other school supplies. ➲

A high headboard separates the bed from the desk area and provides a surface for a reading lamp.

The long, narrow proportions of this room required some clever space-saving solutions. Bunk beds and a built-in wall unit open up floor space. Drawers take the place of a freestanding dresser, while shelves above provide plenty of space for the trappings of youth. ☻

Built-in cabinetry in a warm brown tone borders this bedroom, eliminating the need for freestanding furnishings and storage units. Wooden bins on wheels are a practical way to store toys. When playtime is over, youngsters simply dock the bins into the open areas within the wall unit. 🎧

Sharing a room presents an extra storage challenge. Here, matching built-in dressers—each with two large drawers—are topped with shelves that hold everything from books to baseball caps to toys. A window seat between the dressers features additional drawer storage—a great place for sweatshirts and chunky sweaters. ➲

Colorful and creative, a work- and play station adds an architectural element to this child's bedroom. Disguised as a five-story building, a bookcase divides the workspace into two distinct areas. The smooth, uncluttered surface is ideal for spreading out with books, crafts, or games, while the computer nestles discreetly against the wall. The open shelves are handy for books or display, and a slim shelf below the work surface provides a convenient storage spot. ↑

Though not an official display case, the crossbeam is a perfect spot to show off hard-won trophies.

Within Reach

y keeping **bath accessories** within reach and easily accessible, you can say good-bye to emerging wet from the tub in search of a towel. Built-in cabinetry with open shelving is an excellent way to enhance the functionality and **efficiency** of your bathroom. When quarters are tight, look for creative ways to take advantage of wasted or unused space to gain even a little extra storage. There is no such thing as too much storage in the bathroom.

bright ideas

▶ Expand the capacity of open shelves with storage containers

▶ Remember that baskets, hooks, and pegs are easy for children to use

▶ Extend the vanity countertop to create a useful shelf

Old world charm graces this classic pedestal sink. Just above it, a glass shelf offers a bit of open storage, while the recessed cabinet to the right of the toilet reveals additional shelves. This slender wall unit makes great use of otherwise wasted space. ➲

A handsome antique tub strikes a nostalgic note that encourages long, lingering soaks. Recessed cubbyholes keep towels and other bath accessories tidy and within reach. ⌒

Wall-mounted fixtures are a must when a sink is not set into a countertop. This stylish version has a bit of storage space below, but items used daily, like a toothbrush and a razor, are better kept out in the open. On the adjacent wall, hand towels are draped over a simple towel ring, while a shallow shelved niche keeps toiletries accessible and neatly organized. ➲

Make a style statement with accessories. This toothbrush holder— which echoes the conical shape of the wood vanity—is sleek, yet functional.

Inspired by Arts and Crafts style, this woodwork makes full use of the available space. The floor-to-ceiling unit serves as a vanity, and includes both open and closed storage. A vented cabinet is a convenient hamper—simply discard dirty clothes before slipping into the tub. A dry towel is within arm's reach when it's time to emerge. ☊

This bathroom proves that careful planning can yield storage solutions that are integrated into the overall design of the room. Open shelves with cubbies below allow the bather to reach for a variety of bath amenities, from soaps to natural sponges, without leaving the tub. Along the same wall, a built-in cabinet stows extra towels that create an attractive display through the glass doors. ☊

Closed storage below conceals less attractive items like a hair dryer and cleaning supplies.

Expansive windows in this bathroom bring in natural light, although they limit the opportunity for any type of wall storage. Instead, the tiled tub surround was extended to include a niche designed especially for towels. The surface above serves as a display area for colorful vases and becomes a safe place to sit while drying off and dressing. ➲

Shared Spaces

The bathroom is often the smallest room in the house, yet it is expected to store a vast array of items, from towels and toiletries to dirty laundry and small appliances. When a bathroom is **shared** by two (or more!) people, organization is even more critical—especially around the sink. One smart solution is separate his-and-hers storage for personal effects in addition to a common area for shared items. Think about your storage needs before committing to fixtures.

Though long and narrow, this bathroom features plenty of practical storage. A built-in cabinet that serves as a divider between his-and-her sinks offers easy access to toiletries and such, while cubby-drawers are ideal for accessories and smaller items. The drawers below the counter are shared, while cabinets beneath the sink are strictly off-limits to the other person. This ensures that there's not too much sharing going on! ➲

Around-the-sink accessories make everyday rituals a pleasure. Here, a wall-mounted soap dish and cup holder free up the counter for toiletries, while a lower shelf keeps towels within reach. Another small perch just below the sink holds a few more daily essentials. ☝

Marrying style and substance, this sleek bathroom pairs smooth surfaces with sensible storage. The extended vanity, constructed in a blond wood, houses just one sink, but manages to create two distinct areas with both open and hidden storage. The center cabinet is shared, but drawers on either side are a private affair. ◑

Stowed in symmetrical cubbyholes, towels make a design statement: different colors ensure that there are no mix-ups.

This master bathroom features a modern interpretation of the classic washstand and bowl set between two separate shower stalls. The shower doors are sandblasted glass and provide a measure of privacy, while two slim cabinets on either side of the mirror offer separate storage around the sink. The combination of glass, wood, and stone used throughout the bath is simply stunning. ➲

Freestanding Flexibility

hile most of the fixtures in a bathroom are permanent, this doesn't preclude freestanding furniture from having a place in today's bathrooms. An independent unit is a great way to increase the **functionality** of a bathroom, offering storage and flexibility. Moved in or out as needed, freestanding pieces are ideal for older bathrooms that may lack vanities and tub surrounds. Be flexible and free!

bright ideas

▶ Pair a mirror with a shelf to take the place of a medicine cabinet

▶ Turn an antique table or dresser into a vanity

▶ Enhance spaciousness without sacrificing storage with a floating vanity

Placed on shelves, baskets and other containers help organize and expand the storage possibilities.

This compact, Scandinavian-style cabinet in blond birch offers drawers for storage and a convenient surface for toiletries. The three drawers feature textured glass fronts so that contents can be glimpsed without every detail being revealed. A small mirror above the cabinet turns the piece into a second vanity. ◓

A series of folding bookcases in beech wood are called upon for storage duty in a home spa. Each bookcase consists of three shelves that fold down after the sides have been flipped out. The five bookcases here have been assembled around a large mirror, creating a vanity-like storage area. ◍

Solitude was the primary goal in this bathroom, which features an isolated claw-foot tub. The only addition is a slender antique table, drawn up to the tub's edge to provide a resting place for towels and bath amenities. Wall-mounted towel warmers are waiting on either end when the bather is ready to wrap him- or herself in luxury. ☊

A tub tray is an excellent idea when there is no tub surround.

A traditional pedestal sink is paired with a wood-framed mirror with two hinged leaves. Other unifying touches include a freestanding towel rack positioned near the sink for easy access, and an old-fashioned hamper that folds up for easy relocation. ☉

Here, a simple antique washstand adds old world charm and provides another convenient surface in a lovely bath. ☉

Garage, Attic, and Basement Tips

The garage, attic, and basement are all spaces that have excellent storage potential. If you're lucky enough to have a home with all three, think about placing items that are rarely used—such as memorabilia or toys waiting for the next child—in the attic, and use the garage and basement for more active storage since these spaces are more accessible. Whether you need to find room for a growing wine collection or your home is overflowing with sporting equipment, planning and organization are the keys to turning your garage, attic, and basement into effective storage centers. Below are a few tips to get you started:

Expand storage capacity with freestanding shelf units. Adjustable shelves will allow you to store items of different heights. Stackable crates can also be used in place of shelves for things like paint cans and cleaning products.

Maximize the storage space on the shelves with stackable bins or boxes. Storage containers come in a wide variety of shapes and sizes, and should be labeled for easy identification.

Place smaller, loose items in multiple containers rather than one large box. This is especially helpful when it comes to hardware like nails, which come in various sizes.

Free up floor space by stowing seasonal items like sleds or lawn chairs overhead. In the garage, the space between joists and rafters is ideal.

Keep sporting equipment secure and organized: skis and fishing rods can be stowed upright with dowels to keep them from sliding sideways. Ski poles can be hung directly on the dowels. Bicycles can be hung from their crossbars on brackets mounted on the wall. Store loose items like balls and mitts in a duffel bag that can be hung on a simple hook.

Hang pegboard on the wall to keep tools and gadgets close at hand. Draw an outline of each item onto the pegboard so you'll know where to return it.

Hooks secured to the ceiling or walls can hold a wide range of objects, from folding chairs and cushions to roller blades and ice skates. When placed side by side on the wall, hooks can be used to store longer items such as a patio umbrella.

Make sure all storage spaces are well lit.

Resources

Professional Advice

If you are interested in hiring qualified professionals to help with a remodeling job or new construction, here is a list of design and planning resources that may be helpful:

The National Association of Professional Organizers (NAPO)—A non-profit professional association whose 1200 members include organizing consultants, trainers, and manufacturers of organizing products. NAPO offers a booklet with tips on getting organized, and a referral service. www.napo.net

The National Closet Group (NCG)—A network of independent closet companies throughout the country. Its website offers helpful consumer tips and a free locator service. www.nationalclosetgroup.com

American Institute of Architects (AIA)—When making structural changes, an architect should be considered. Many, but not all, architects belong to the American Institute of Architects. Call (202) 626-7300 for information and the phone number of your local chapter. www.aiaonline.com

The American Society of Interior Designers (ASID)—An interior designer can provide helpful advice, especially when remodeling an existing space. The American Society of Interior Designers represents over 20,000 professionally qualified interior designers. Call ASID's client/referral service at (800) 775-ASID. www.asid.org

The National Kitchen and Bath Association (NKBA)—The National Kitchen and Bath Association certifies kitchen designers (CKD). They can provide full-service project management or design services only. Call (800) 401-NKBA, extension 665, for a list of designers near you, or write for more information: NKBA, 687 Willow Grove Street, Hackettstown, NJ 07840. The NKBA website is also an excellent general resource for information: www.nkba.com

National Association of the Remodeling Industry (NARI)—When it's time to select a contractor to work on your project, you might consider a member of the National Association of the Remodeling Industry. Call (800) 611-6274 for more information. www.nari.org

National Association of Home Builders (NAHB)—When you're looking at builders to construct a new home, contact the National Association of Home Builders. Call (800) 368-5242 for more information. www.nahb.org

Other Resources

The following manufacturers, associations, and resources may be helpful with finding your storage solutions:

HOME FURNISHINGS AND ACCESSORIES

Arhaus
(866) 427-4287
www.arhaus.com

Baker Furniture
(800) 59 BAKER
www.bakerfurniture.com

Century Furniture
(828) 328-1851
www.centuryfurniture.com

Charles P. Rogers Beds
(800) 272-7726
www.charlesprogers.com

Crate&Barrel
(800) 967-6696
www.crateandbarrel.com

Design Within Reach
(800) 967-0411
www.dwr.com

Ethan Allen
(203) 743-8000
www.ethanallen.com

Harden Furniture
(315) 245-1000
www.harden.com

Home Depot
(770) 433-8211
www.homedepot.com

Ikea
(315) 245-1000
www.ikea.com

JCPenney
(800) 222-6161
www.jcpenney.com

Lands' End
(800) 963-4816
www.landsend.com

Lexington Home Furnishings
(800) 539-4636
www.lexington.com

Lillian Vernon
(800) 285-5555
www.lillianvernon.com

L.L. Bean
(800) 441-5713
www.llbean.com

Pottery Barn
(800) 922-5507
www.potterybarn.com

Pottery Barn Kids
(800) 430-7373
www.potterybarnkids.com

Room & Board
(800) 486-6554
www.roomandboard.com

Sauder Furniture
(800) 523-3987
www.sauder.com

Sears
(800) 549-4505
www.sears.com

Spiegel
(800) SPIEGEL
www.spiegel.com

Target
(888) 304-4000
www.target.com

Thomasville
(800) 927-9202
www.thomasville.com

KITCHEN CABINETRY

Aristokraft
(812) 482-2527
www.aristokraft.com

KraftMaid
(800) 249-4321
www.kraftmaid.com

Merillat
(517) 263-0771
www.merillat.com

Plain & Fancy
(800) 447-9006
www.plainfancycabinetry
.com

Wellborn
(800) 336-8040
www.wellborncabinet.com

Wood-Mode
(800) 635-7500
www.wood-mode.com

ORGANIZATION AND STORAGE SOLUTIONS

California Closets
(800) 336-9189
www.calclosets.com

Container Store
(800) 733-3532
www.containerstore.com

Hold Everything
(800) 840-3596
www.holdeverything.com

Storage by Design
(877) 772-2313
www.customclosets.com

Valet Closet
(800) 447-1041

Photo Credits

Beateworks/beateworks.com: ©Tim Street Porter, 16–17 (Architect: Frank Israel), 55 right, 76 (Designer: Barbara Barry), 108, 115; ©Eric Staudenmaier, 17 right (Media case Architect/Designer: Rachel Vert)
©**Steven Brooke:** 53 bottom, 83
California Closets: 124
The Container Store: 31, 105
©**Crandall & Crandall:** 68 (Builder: Ron Holden, Holden Construction), 72 (Builder: Judy Ramazzina and Werner Berry, Home Improvement Specialists)
Crate&Barrel: ©Steven McDonald, 30, 36, 42, 49, 64, 120, 121
©**Carlos Domenech:** 86
Elizabeth Whiting Associates: 38 bottom, 39, 93 top; ©Jon Bouchier, 74; ©Andreas von Einsiedel, 22 top, 22 bottom; ©Brian North, 14 left ; ©Ian Parry, 38 top; ©Friedhelm Thomas, 23
©**Everett & Soulé Architectural Photographers:** 14–15 (Designer: David Pearson Design)
©**Tria Giovan:** 10, 24 top, 37, 96–97, 99
©**Gross & Daley:** 52, 53 top, 106 left
©**Nancy Hill:** 26 (Designer: Deborah T. Lipner), 65 bottom (Designer: Kitchens by Deane), 113 (Designer: Stirling Design Associates)

Houses & Interiors: ©Jake Fitzjones, 96 left (Designer: Simon Horn Beds)
Interior Archive: ©Tim Beddow, 60–61 (Designer: Melissa Stephenson), 122 (Designer: Melissa Stephenson); ©Tim Clinch, 77 (Architect: Piers Gough); ©Eduardo Munoz, 24 bottom (Architect: David Mikhail); ©Ed Reeve, 88 (Architect: Julian de Metz), 89 (Architect: Julian de Metz); ©Ianthe Ruthven, 92 (Architect: Charles Jencks); ©Simon Upton, 65 top (Designer: Jonathan Grey), 123 top (Designer: Ilaria Miani); ©Wayne Vincent, 78 left; ©Henry Wilson, 41 (Architect: John Pawson); ©Andrew Wood, 18–19 (Architect: Spencer Fung), 19 right (Architect: Spencer Fung), 58 (Stylist: Polly Dickens), 84 (Stylist: Polly Dickens), 102 (Designer: Jayne Wunder)
©**Rob Melnychuk:** 56, 78–79, 87, 94, 95, 118
©**Peter Paige:** 106–107 (Designer: Adam Tihany)
©**Tim Street Porter:** 11, 45 right (Designer: Barbara Barry), 70 top (Designer: Jan Weimer), 70 bottom (Designer: Jan Weimer), 71 top (Designer: Jan Weimer)
©**Undine Prohl:** 12–13 (Architect: David Baker), 13 right (Architect: David Baker), 85 (Architect: Brian

MacKay-Lyons), 91 (Architect: Leddy/Maytum/Stacy)
Red Cover: ©Andreas von Einsiedel, 101 (Interior Designer: Patrice Nourissat), 103 (Interior Designer: Jorge Villon), 112 (Interior Designer: Jorge Villon); ©Jake Fitzjones, 75 left; ©Ken Hayden, 40 (Designer: Michael Reeves), 59 (Designers: David and Pamela Furze), 119 (Designer: Kelly Hoppen); ©Huntley Hedworth, 54–55; ©Andrew Twort, 51 top
©**Eric Roth:** 57, 104, 110
©**Mark Samu:** 2 (Architect: Brian Shore; Stylist: Luciana Samu), 34–35 (Stylist: Margaret McNicholas), 46 (Designer: Luciana Samu; Stylist: Margaret McNicholas), 50–51 bottom (Architect: Brian Shore; Stylist: Tia Burns), 67 (Stylist: Margaret McNicholas), 73 (Architect: EJR Associates; Stylist: Tia Burns), 75 right (Stylist: Margaret McNicholas), 80 (Stylist: Margaret McNicholas), 81 (Stylist: Margaret McNicholas), 82 (Designer: Eileen Boyd; Stylist: Margaret McNicholas), 98 (Architect: Brian Shore; Stylist: Luciana Samu), 111 (Stylist: Margaret McNicholas), 116 (Stylist: Margaret McNicholas), 123 bottom (Stylist: Margaret McNicholas)

©**Brad Simmons:** 44–45 (Architect: Robert Gordon; Builder: Original Log Homes), 117 (Builder: Town & Country Cedar Homes)
©**Brian Vanden Brink:** 6 (Architect: Weston & Hewiston), 20–21 (Architect: Elliott & Elliott), 25 (Architect: Mark Hutker & Associates), 27 (Architect: Thom Rouselle), 32–33 (Architect: John Gillespie), 34 left (Architect: Alan Frysinger; Interior Designer: Christina Oliver), 43 (Architect: Alan Frysinger), 47, 48 (Architect: Elliott & Elliott), 69 left, 69 right, 90 left, 90 right, 100 left (Architect: Van Dam & Renner), 100 right (Architect: Alan Frysinger), 109 (Architect: Weston & Hewiston), 114 (Architect: Weston & Hewiston)
©**Jessie Walker:** 28–29 (Designer: The Workshops of David T. Smith; Stylist: Aurelia Joyce Pace), 62 (Architect: Mastro & Skylar), 63 (Architect: Mastro & Skylar), 66 (Designer: Gail Drury, CKD, CBD, Drury Design), 71 bottom (Designer: Gail Drury, CKD, CBD, Drury Design), 93 bottom (Designer: The Cornerstone Studio; Stylist: Aurelia Joyce Pace)

Index

Athletic gear, 8, 124
Attic space, 100, *100*, 124
Audio components, 13, *13*, 14, *15*
Basement space, 124
Baskets, *18*, 19, 20
  bathroom, 110
  below the counter, 53, *53*
  kitchen, 64, *64*
  nesting, 24, *24*
  outerwear, 44, *44*
  tea, 75, *75*
  wicker, 53, *53*, 75, *75*
  wire, 75, *75*, 105, *105*
Bathrooms, 9, 110–123
  accessories, 112, *112*, 117, *117*
  cabinets, 110, *110*, 112, *112*, 113, *113*, 116, *116*, 120, 121, *121*
  fixtures, 110, *110*, 111, *111*, 112, *112*, 122, *122*, 123, *123*
  hampers, 113, *113*, 123, *123*
  vanities, 113, *113*, 118, *118*, 119, 120
Bedrooms, 9, 84–103
  bookcases, 85, *85*
  closets, 98–103
  display space in, 84
  dressers, 99, *99*
  headboards, 85, *85*, 104, *104*, 106, 107
  master, 88
  nightstands, 84, 87, *87*
  sharing, 108, *109*
  sleeping lofts, 88, 90, *90*, 92, *92*, 93, *93*
  televisions in, 86, *86*
Beds
  bunk, 106, *106*
  captain's, 91, *91*
  daybeds, 90, *90*
  Murphy, 88, *88*, 89, *89*, 96, 97
  platform, 94, 95, *95*
  sleigh, 96, *96*
  trundle, 88

Benches
  storage under, 42
Bins, 20, *21*
  color-coded, 104
  stackable, 124
  trash, 66
  on wheels, 107, *107*
Bookcases, 8, *16*, 17, 69, *69*, 85, *85*, 94, 95
  children's, 108, *108*
  curved, 30, *30*
  floor-to-ceiling, 20, *21*, 23, *23*
  pocket doors and, 24, *24*
Boxes, *18*, 19, 20
  nesting, 40, *40*
  stackable, 124
Cabinets, 114, *114*
  base, 56, 57, 60–61, 61
  bathroom, 110, *110*, 112, *112*, 113, *113*, 116, *116*, 120, 121, *121*
  built-in, 107, *107*, 114, *114*
  closed, 52, *52*
  custom, 50, 100, *100*
  floor-to-ceiling, 96, 97, *113*, *113*
  foldout, 69, *69*
  glass, 26, *26*
  glass-front, 35, *35*, 51, *51*, 52, *52*, 56, 57, 82, *82*
  hardware, 50, 53, *53*
  kitchen, 50–57
  media, 10, *10*, 86, *86*
  open-through, 57, *57*
  overhead, 34, *34*
  pull-out, 22, *22*, 74, 75
  pull-out shelves in, 14, *14*
  recessed, 110, *110*
  sliding, 67, *67*
  space over, 68, *68*
  stepped base, 54, *54*
  stock, 50
  suspended, 57, *57*
  vented, 113, *113*
  vertical division, 50, 71, *71*
  wall-to-wall, 85, *85*

Carts
  drop-leaf, 64, *64*
  prep, 59, *59*
Ceilings
  high, 52, *52*, 93
Children's rooms, 104–109
Closets, 98–103
  floor-to-ceiling, *18*, 19, 41, *41*
  half-height rails, 98, *98*, 99, *99*
  walk-in, 8
Clothing, 9
Coat racks, 44, *44*
Coffee tables, 13
Collections, 26–31, 80, *80*
Computers, 36, *36*, 37, *37*, 105, 108, *108*
Corkboard, 32, 81
Countertops, 60–61, *61*, 62, *62*
  butcher-block, 65, *65*
  curved, 54, *54*
  desk, 34, *34*
  granite, 55, *55*
  heights, 65
  knife slot, 65, *65*
  laundry, 46, *46*, 48, 49
  lighting, 82, *82*
  L-shaped, 35, *35*
Cubbies, 43, *43*
  bathroom, 114, *114*
  closet, 99, *99*
  recessed, 111, *111*
Desks, 11, *11*, 36, *36*, 37, *37*, 40, 41, *41*
  built-in, 34, *34*
  children's, 104, *104*, 105, *105*
  kitchen, 70, *70*
Doors
  glass, 11
  opaque, 20
  sliding, 13, *13*, 31, *31*, 79, *79*, 82, *82*
Doorways
  space above, 26

Drawers, 9, *18*, 19, 56, 57
  bedroom, 84, 87, *87*
  built-in, 41, *41*, 106, *106*
  chopping board, 67, *67*
  compost, 64, *65*
  cubby, 81, *81*
  cutlery, 66
  divided, 71, *71*
  hanging file, 32, 34, *34*
  kitchen, 51, *51*, 64, *64*
  knife, 65, *65*, 71, *71*
  metal-lined, 72, *72*
  nightstand, 84
  refrigerated, 73, *73*
  trash, 66
  two-tiered, 66
  under the bed, 91, *91*, 94, 95, *95*, 96, *96*
  wicker, 37, *37*
Dressers, 99, *99*, 100, *100*
  built-in, 108, *109*
  matching, 108, *109*
Entertainment centers, 10–19
  built-in, 8
  freestanding, 13, *13*
  pullout shelf, 11, *11*
Entryways, 42
  coat hooks in, 44, *44*
Garage space, 124
Garment racks, 49, *49*
Headboards, 85, *85*, 104, *104*, 106, 107
Home offices, 8, 32–41
  location, 35
Hooks
  bathroom, 110
  clothing, 98, *99*
  coat, 44, *44*
  cup, 76, *76*
Kitchens, 8
  appliance garage, 53, *53*, 66, *67*
  commercial, 59
  desks, 70, *70*
  drop-leaf cart, 64, *64*
  galley, 59, *59*

islands, *50, 51, 55, 55, 58,*
59, 65
L-shape, 51, *51*
peninsulas, 52, *52*
prep carts, 59, *59*
shelves, 54, *54*
utensil and cookware storage, 58–70
work centers, 58–65
work triangle in, 50
Laundry areas, 42, 46, *46,*
47, 47, 48, 49, 49
Lazy Susan trays, 66
Library ladders, 20, *21*
Lighting
accent, 50
ceiling, 92, *92*
desk lamps, 36, *36,* 37, *37,*
40, *40*
natural, 78, *78,* 102, *102,*
115
reading, 87, *87*
sconces, 92, *92*
spotlights, 28, 29
work area, 82, *82*
Magazine racks, 84
Mirrors
bathroom, 123, *123*
closet, 98, *98*
Mudrooms, 42, 43, *43*
heated floors, 42
Nightstands, 84, 87, *87*
Ottomans, *12,* 13
Pantries, *60–61, 61,* 74, 75,
75
butler's, 80–83

foldout, 72
Potting areas, 46, *46*
Racks
coat, 44, *44*
magazine, 84
overhead, 58
shoe, 98
tie, 98
towel, 66, 122, *122,* 123, *123*
wine, 55, *55*
Railings, utensil-hanging,
60–61, 61
Room dividers, 30, *30,* 78,
78, 84, *84,* 94, 95, *95*
Shelves, 9, 20–25
adjustable, 20, 105, *105,*
124
baskets for, 20, 24, *24*
boxes for, 20
built-in, 14, *15,* 20, 25, *25,*
26, 27, 41, *41,* 104, *104*
display, 55, *55*
floor-to-ceiling, 23, *23*
freestanding, 124
glass, 11, 53, *53,* 78, *78,*
110, *110*
heights, 24
industrial-style, 17, *17*
kitchen, 54, *54*
lift-up, 58
open, *18,* 19, *26, 27, 31, 31,*
51, 51, 59, 59, 75, 75, 78,
78, 79, 79, 80, *80,* 83,
83, 84, *84, 85, 85,* 99,
99, 108, *108,* 114, *114,*
121, *121*

painted, 20
pullout, 14, *14,* 58, 66
recessed, 20, 67, *67*
self-feeding, 72
shallow, 11, 26, *60–61, 61,*
112, *112*
sliding, 63, *63*
staggered, 76, *76*
swing-out, 68, *68*
vertical, 37, *37*
wall-mounted, 105, *105*
wheeled, 84, *84*
wire, 42
Stairs
spiral, 23, *23*
Storage
auxiliary, 80–83
bathroom, 110–123
bedroom, 84–103
beneath-stair, 22, *22*
built-in, 92, *92*
children's, 104–109
closed, 9, 10, 35, *35,* 45, *45,*
80, *80*
clothing, 98–103
decorative, 26–31
food, 72–75
home entertainment,
10–19
home office, 32–41
kitchen, 50–80
media, 10–19
open, 9, 32, 40, *40,*
76–79
ornamental, 26–31
as part of room design, 9

space-saving, 66–71,
88–97
stairway, 22, *22,* 23, *23,* 25,
25
toy, 104, 107, *107*
under the bed, 88
utility areas, 42–49
wine, 55, *55,* 81, *81,* 82, *82,*
83, *83*
Televisions, 10, 13, *13,* 16, *17,*
18, 19
Toiletries, 9, 110, *110,* 112,
112
Towel racks, 66
Trunks, 103, *103*
Utility areas, 42–47
VCRs, 10, 16, 17
Walls
curved, 76, 77
undulating, *16,* 17
Wall units, 17, *17*
built-in, 106, *106*
custom, 10
media, 10
modular, 10, 20
open, 40, *40*
Wardrobes, 103, *103*
Wet bars, 26, 27
Windows
circular, 92, *92*
space above, 26, *26*
Window seats, 14, *14,* 93, *93,*
108, *109*
Wine storage, 55, *55,* 81, *81,*
82, *82,* 83, *83,* 124
Workspaces, 32–41, 80–83,
108, *108*